The Portable Famine

ALSO BY RANE ARROYO

The Portable Famine

Rane Arroyo

Winner of the John Ciardi Prize for Poetry
selected by Robin Becker

BkMk Press
University of Missouri-Kansas City

BkMk Press
University of Missouri-Kansas City
5101 Rockhill Road
Kansas City, Missouri 64110
(816) 235-2558 (voice)
(816) 235-2611 (fax)
bkmk@umkc.edu
www.umkc.edu/bkmk

Cover photographs: Jennifer Echavarria
Book design: Jennifer Echavarria and Susan L. Schurman
Associate Editor: Michelle Boisseau
Managing Editor: Ben Furnish
Printing: Walsworth Publishing Company, Marceline, Missouri

BkMk Press wishes to thank Adriana Arteaga, Bill Beeson, Heather Clark, Dennis Conrow, Sandra K. Davies, David E. Rowe.

The John Ciardi Prize for Poetry wishes to thank Susan Cobin, Greg Field, Steve Gehrke, Jeannie M. Irons, Elaine K. Lally, Michael Nelson, Linda Rodriguez, Maryfrances Wagner.

Previous winners of the John Ciardi Prize for Poetry:
    The Resurrection Machine by Steve Gehrke, selected by Miller Williams
    Kentucky Swami by Tim Skeen, selected by Michael Burns
    Escape Artist by Terry Blackhawk, selected by Molly Peacock
    Fence Line by Curtis Bauer, selected by Christopher Buckley

Library of Congress Cataloging-in-Publication Data
Arroyo, Rane.
    The portable famine : poetry / by Rane Arroyo
        p. cm.
    "2004 John Ciardi Poetry Prize winner"
    Summary: "The portable famine offers poems from Rane Arroyo's years of being an 'interior exile' as a gay, Puerto Rican, and Midwestern writer whose travels have taken him throughout American cities such as Chicago, Miami, New York, New Orleans, Pittsburgh, and Toledo; the European cities of Florence, London, and Reykjavík; and locations across the Carribean, including Puerto Rico"—Provided by publisher.
    ISBN 1886157537 (pbk.: alk. paper) 1. Voyages and travels—Poetry. 2. Puerto Ricans—Poetry. 3. Middle West—Poetry. 4. Gay men—poetry. 5. Poetry of places. I. Title.
    PS3551 .R722 P67   2005
    811'. 54--dc22

                          2005021012

This book is set in Jenson Pro, ITC Tiepolo, and Parisian type.

When Rane Arroyo declares, "Even in imaginary America,/ America has to be imagined," he signals the magical transports these poems enact. They bristle with geography—New York, San Juan, London, Provo, Reykjavík, Tijuana, Miami—and delight with innovation. His narrators, border-crossers in every sense, take up diaspora as a central theme: "Will any place actually be mine?" one asks. Lovers and family members and solitudes populate these pages, along with the beloved artists (Arenas, Blake, Neruda, O'Hara) who accompany the poet on his literal and metaphysical travels.

"I'm the shore/of their shore leaves," the speaker claims in "Saturday Night in San Juan with the Right Sailors," illustrating his signature, linguistic playfulness. Erotic, irreverent, mournful, political, Arroyo's lyrics and narratives surprise, often by juxtaposing literary erudition and popular culture within the same stanza. The result is a hybrid poetics all his own. Read his arguments, direct addresses, dream poems, elegies, family narratives, and love poems to experience an incisive, original mind exploring "the square roots of restlessness."

—Robin Becker
Judge, John Ciardi Prize for Poetry

ACKNOWLEDGMENTS

I'm honored to be in the company and part of the community of past and future winners of the John Ciardi Poetry Prize.

Some of these poems were previously published, often under different titles and as earlier versions, in the following magazines whose dedication to words inspire readers and writers:

Confrontation
Gargoyle
The Hampden-Sydney Poetry Review
The Hawaii Review
Heliotrope
Into the Teeth of the Wind
The Louisville Review
The Massachusetts Review
Midwest Miscellany
The Mochila Review
Off The Rocks
PoetryMagazine.com
Pool
Potomac Review
Quarterly West
Riverwind.

"The Burrito King of Toledo, Ohio" was published in *The Ohioana Quarterly* and featured in the Thurber House as part of the Ohio Bicentennial celebration.

"Almost A Revolution For Two In Bed" and "Saturday Night In San Juan With The Right Sailors" are included in the ground-breaking *A Fi We Time: Contemporary Caribbean Lesbian and Gay Writing*, Duke University Press, an anthology edited by Thomas Glave.

"The Immigrants (Winter Wear)" was the 2004 winning poem of the Gwendolyn Brooks Poetry Prize from the Society for the Study of Midwestern Literature.

The Portable Famine

CONTENTS

Dedicated to Glenn, Little Bee
and my illegal extended familia.

Also I wish for us all to remember and honor
the poet Charles Henri Ford.

The aim of their existence was not mine;
My joys, my griefs, my passions, and my powers
Made me a stranger

Lord Byron, *Manfred*

THE SINGER ENRIQUE IGLESIAS
AS MY MUSE IN THESE TROUBLED TIMES

Enrique, you and I swim in a pool on
the Empire State Building's rooftop. How

far from sharks must we be? forever?
Clouds turn into steppingstones.

Suddenly, we're in Babylon and you
take off my gold cross, hide it in your

mouth. Questioned, we are stripped
and painted the red of Puerto Rican

roosters. Bees carry you to God. I limp
home where you somehow wait wearing

flesh again. We compare morning beards.
Music yields to the yes underneath breath.

We exchange shadows, glow without
greed and let winged goats eat the roof.

TOO ALONE IN METROPOLIS

It's snowing. The flakes look
like atoms puffed up against
enemies. A zillion Adams

have come and gone, and it's
my turn at the wheel of fortune as,
under streetlights, snowflakes

are magnets attracting each other.
Then they plunge into the black,
this world's mirror. White nights—

some spent reading, some misspent
in semen, some sent to the mind
as dreams of icebergs, ghosts, sky's

glass skull, transparent shadows.
Just under my white ceiling,
an avalanche tests its wings.

THREE LATINOS, ONE CITY

Daniel, thrown out by your parents
and their puffed santos, you who thrived
secretly in a storage locker palace
after salsa clubs, handsome heartbreak:
have I missed your obituary?

Arturo, blinded author, the one who says
"imagine—only a small part of this
continent has been graced by parrots."
You will replace the sky with your books.
Dismissed as an AIDS Chihuahua
junkyard dog, you laugh without permission.

Libaye, amigo, my magnetic New York has
always been about post-Eden deaths: those
unscripted SIDA sideshows. Now, one by one,

writers are also vanishing. For example,
Charles Henri Ford. This Boriqueño and
boyfriend had tea with him and Indra in

the Dakota of John Lennon's assassination.
Charles was a prophet still gossiping about
Peggy Guggenheim. He's gone, another urban

ghost. Even realized buildings unthread,
yield to historical forces that may steal your
youth long before you can misspend it.

LITTLE SONG FOR A BIG DEATH

Mourning is abstract until it's not.
Then it moves in, then it unpacks.

Then it puts on your shoes, pants, hats,
lifelines. It opens your mail, diaries.

It makes collect calls on dead phones.
Mourning borrows our secret flaws

and cheapens them into parades.
It's the magnifying glass that

theater is not, tears becoming blindfolds.
It's a map of sinking islands,

a globe outliving human names.
It feeds on sentimentality, like when

a sugary song makes you pull over
and weep: *la, la, la, if I had you.*

DETAILS AS REVELATIONS

It's my turn to buy the condoms.
The cashier blushes at the possibilities
we've been conquering. I also buy

bleach, a toy mouse for the cat, underwear
for you to take off me. We don't talk
about a future. The street shines with

mannequins in rhinestone. We walk
as if just friends. We stop at Big Books
and there is a sale on literary critics,

half-off. You know before foreplay
there is foreplay, the mind's turn to
ride shotgun. We end up at *Pearlia's*

for a happy hour populated by extras
from Dracula: The Musical. Off-off-off
Broadway isn't a real neighborhood.

CNN is overthrown by the jukebox.
We compare passports, gods, and shoe
deals. You want to be seen. With me!

I'm not sure why. We talk about nothing
as if it's everything. We order a last round
to hurry back to my room, to a happiness.

MAYBERRY, RFD

Not even one illegal Mexican
in the body shop? No Guatemalan
maid at One Hour Motel? Not

a Puertorriqueña owning
a Tex-Mex restaurant? How
white *is* white? Poor Opie,

taught to fear jalapeños.
Even in imaginary America,
America has to be imagined.

DREAMING IN TEXAS

I still have nightmares of Hansel
and Gretel. That moving sidewalk
of crumbs. The witch forced to work
overtime. The unloved oven. History

yawns. Another night: Hansel is gay
and a slumlord, Sodom's dark side.
Gretel sells blind dolls over the Internet.
Conservatives force me to choose one for

my shotgun wedding. I wake up to dream
again: The witch peddles her memoirs,
Texas Black Tea and Me and The Hunger.
I've been footnoted. Hansel and Gretel

are winkers who brag about their boots.
That new dream fades, but others seduce:
I'm in glowing Germany and Jews are
firewood. Then, I'm at Jack Kennedy's

bachelor party. Gretel is stripping.
She's edible. Hansel is the men's room
attendant writing poems on toilet paper.
Texas is generous with blackouts.

Next, a cartoon's atom bomb straightens
the witch's curls. We're all orphans.
Hansel and Gretel hold my hands
as we skip back to the burning city.

MY BRIEF NEW ORLEANS

A black mother leaves her girl
to cry on the sidewalk, her shoes
on her hands instead of her feet.

Oh, if you were my daughter, baby,
I'd be the terrors I've fled most
of my life. Embraces would never end.

I'd build Barbie's dream White House.
I'd never lend you to school. I'd be
a father from Hell, taking all the bullets,

dying again and again until you'd
get bored with my simplicity. I'd bake
cookies shaped like conclusions, wear

your scent as oxygen's only true rival.
How you'd tire of me, my impossible girl,
for leaving lights on—even at noon.

No voodoo queen told my future.
I did not crawl Bourbon Street with
any versions of Tennessee Williams'

shades, did not feed drunks shaking off
well-scrubbed hometowns. And yet
New Orleans has followed me here

to snow country. Not its vampires,
shirtless jocks, erudite bouncers, or
slave quarters turned into bed-and-

breakfast palaces. No, a sadness
is here, an unscripted hangover of other
people's desires in a city doomed

to perpetual adolescence. Don't worry,
New Orleans, rest and take a bath here,
grin without needing a conquest in sight.

CREATURES

My sister tells of panthers in her
panting Florida backyard. I'm back
to editing *Diary of a Pet Snake.*
The sex scenes are clumsy and slow—why?

"Delilah After Dark" features
Dixie who loves her transvestite twin
no matter what. Innocence won't stop
giving the world its toothy grins.

I wonder if "extra-large" on underwear
packages is merely froth. Letters are
the secret ribs of creatures we cannot
destroy. There never was a Noah.

A TERRIBLE BEAUTY

Miami is the mating ground
for plastic pink flamingos

that may yet nest in our souls.
The sun turns us into treasures—for?

We're punch-drunk rum dreamers,
holy sinners—when we're lucky,

when our bodies are the books
spilling alphabets without fear.

Bars fill up with Babylonian
émigrés and empire builders.

Forget Yeats' swans. We've pink
flamingos as our holy doves.

O America, the astonisher!
O city of expensive mirages!

Sí, convert us, coiffed Havana
wannabe, into dancing sleepwalkers.

RETURNING TO PUERTO RICO
AS A STRANGER

Sunlight offers relentless kisses
until the hotel's plaza goes blind,
its poured-concrete gargoyles stilled

in their nostalgia for vague España.
Jíbaros gossip before aging tourists
saddled with cameras. Church bells

only offer one season: martyrdom.
Whited houses turn their backs to
the pearl-poor sea. There is so much

I didn't pack the first time I left, and
still can't. Men with fingerprints on proud
foreheads sing, *escape your prayers.*

This place is a crime scene without a crime.
This fever is a camel courted by oases.
The dead don't care about my family roots,

but they do envy my daily running about.
They send me a moon without a translator.
I won't waste my powers on dreaming.

PARADISE RECLAIMED

Lacking the intimacy of a jealous god,
we trust the lifeguards in their towers to cry out

shark, shark, with the voice of a cantor.
The cabana boys run for the red umbrellas

testing their wings against the black arrival of
uninformed winds. Logic courses never heal.

It's the past that is our enemy, that hunger for
piracy long after flotillas have been plucked.

We are doomed with the geopolitical spaces
of desire: the surface of this planet as the only

archaeological site for Eden. The road to Atlantis
is clogged with coral the color of old blood.

The cabana boys gather to talk about their tips
as if the future's portents, their bodies as prayers

that have nothing to do with founding religions.
Footprints in the sand are drafts of love letters.

SATURDAY NIGHT IN SAN JUAN WITH THE RIGHT SAILORS

I'm younger than the calendar. We like this
floating on bar stools, mermen amazed by
our miraculous sea legs. Apocalypse has

nothing to offer, upstaged as it is by this
jukebox playing Shakira—as if noise staves off
dawn. They rub against me for I'm the shore

of their shore leaves. It's just before the heat
leads to choices, and we like this competition
between beers and our fate lines, the risks.

24

DIASPORA: A SUMMARY

there is too much nothing here
    —Derek Walcott, "Air"

We step off the hard island,
but it doesn't stay where it is.
We seek eloquence's soft hands
and also skies different than

those that veil our family graves.
We always plan on returning,
to plant our feet on the raw shores
of our blood source with news

to cure our burnt island of the raw
darkness about to wear a volcano,
the darkness that is the topics. Long
long distance calls are drowned out

by seagulls' doxologies. It's hard
to believe that even continents float
and that the past was our past on
an island rowing away from us.

Scattering is not yet perfected for
we must return *home* to mourn,
blood ties unknotting. Again, we've
faces naked with tears and sea salt.

ALMOST A REVOLUTION
FOR TWO IN BED

You're still the island of the holy
palm tree. What can I offer to the man
married first to God and then soon to
the wrong rib? Here, it's shining outside,
a spy stirred by the colors between us.
The sea is never rhetorical and asks
about your nakedness, that theater.

You weep because your clothes
drag you back to vows. I will not
comfort you, not be another goddamn
mosquito net for Adam's innocents,
not shave this dawn's whiskers of
whispers. Coconuts look the balls
of angels refusing perfection.

You leave. I stay. We fall off
the bed, this time as ghosts.
Winds steal words from books.
In the mirror, I see verbs,
read Arenas' Arenas, discover
love letters inside my irises,
rediscover Homer's honesty:
we return to our leavings.

WHY I HATE PITTSBURGH #1

for Julie Parson-Nesbitt

Sunday morning and I
stand before a statue of Pan.
Is he loving Humanity?
a choreographed rape?

Pan has no dramatic crotch,
or else it has been taken
away by the city's leading
eunuchs. One jogger eyes

a boy sketching the horizon
of trees. Jesus, it's too
early to prey. Pan is bored,
having seen and done it all.

Birds eat off his untroubled
head. Oh-oh, the jogger
is eyeing me now. I'm no mucho
macho off-duty. Fortunately life

isn't a poem and I can walk out
of here. Goodbye, Pan,
you never were holy, were you?
Actually the opaque figleaf

makes you look like Andrew
Carnegie's go-go boyfriend.
A cop thinks I may be illegal,
but I'm looking at statues—I'm

human. Pittsburgh would crush
my head instead of wine grapes or
strikes. There are so many ways to
celebrate steel stealing our souls.

THE VISITOR

el pan azul de cada día
[each day's blue bread]
–Pablo Neruda, "The Thrush Warbled, Pure Bird."

You're dead, but your skies are not.
This Ohio storm makes me think of your
blackening Chilean horizons. What use

is your name now in the not-now,
not-here? Neruda. Ne. Ruda. Neru.
Da. It was a wonderful mask, no?

Pablito, there is a spider in my spinning
bedroom with blind rubies for eyes.
Is this a message from you? Dawn is

still painful, old amigo, and pain is
always a vague ghost nostalgic for
the blue bread that we eat to forget

our missing talent for love. The dead
have mud for skies, ¿no? Imagine, poet,
we can incorporate, sell shares in ourselves!

Sí, the world is still extraliterary. Are there
bakers in the afterlife? Poetry asks for you
by name, the one finally yours. Stop grinning.

"I'M NOT A FEMINIST, BUT. . ."

for Jaimie Barlowe

Reading Ovid in a Midwest heat wave,
I wince at how many women are
punished for their beauty. This is

the era of the mini bikini, the only
gift the atomic bomb has brought to
the darkening ages. These days,

we do not turn girls into cows,
trees or constellations—except
in Hollywood. We also airbrush

supermodels so they have no links
to apes, Christmas tree virgins or
witches with legs locked on brooms

that rivals turn into crosses. Instead
of transformations, we have daytime
makeovers. Instead of Jove and

his jealous wife, we have celebrity
scandals. Our silicone nuns wage
war against time and the mirror.

The heat index is 110° and we are
still worried about appearances, still
overdressed in myths without mercy.

THE IMMIGRANTS (WINTER WEAR)

They are, at first, scared of snowmen.
Of the snow and the white men
so easily born between the hands of

children veiled in breaths and winter wear.
The immigrants worry about bodies
built without concerns for their souls,

about this strange country in which food
is so plentiful that carrots are used
for noses. White pillars are made by

tall chimneys. No wonder that furry
Santa Claus has replaced Jesus of
the desert: boots needed, as are hats

and vague drinks like vodka or gin. Rum
is too allied with the sun and the sugar
of any rotting calendar. This freezing

is a funeral before there is a corpse.
Snowballs take on the shape of baby skulls.
Snow angels need no documentations.

Enough, it's over: back to thawing kitchens
full of chiles and recipes requiring all
that won't grow in this version of tundra.

Seal up the goddamn windows with
steam, says an old woman, this is no cruise,
there is nothing to see. Crows fly across

MEMOIRS: CHICAGO POEMS

After John F. Kennedy Isn't Our Savior

What a strange country in which white
men kill each other. What hope is
there that the rest of us aren't targets?

"Ramón, you're too curious," Mami sighs.
Sí, but she hasn't been slapped for failing
to write the letter R with long enough legs.

"Raymond," the teacher hisses, "that's a P."
Perhaps it's best to hide in plain sight.
I respond to Raymond, write perfect R's.

❧

Papi Says That I'm Dead, But I'm Not

I was allowed to walk one dark block
to the blinking American store to buy
candy from Mexico. Mami watched
to make sure I wasn't kidnapped—by?

The past is raised, but not razed, as small
moments survive epiphany. Papi searched
TV for Spanish programs and settled
for *Fantasy Island*. My body wasn't

a true passport yet. I was bought maps of
states which I'd stick to the cracking ceiling.
Finally, light years later, I went away when
my dark pubic hair became bold oars.

❧

Skipper

Mami dreams that only she and I
see her dead dog returned as
a puppy. How many times do we
have to start a new life in America?

Bankruptcy, religions, lovers, and
airports are fake antidotes to our
illogical lives, illusions. I was there
to pet Skipper while he was injected

with a liquid sharing the color of the sea.
I only offer Mami comfort, a uselessness
akin to cemetery statues with wings
and mock feet stuck in local mud.

Let her dream: it's all that I know
of resurrection, of a dead dog returned
to us as a puppy unconcerned with
what vanishes without ceremony.

Dark Anniversary

I hate it when ghosts make you guess
who they were.
　　　　O, it's you, Uncle, but
I'd rather haunt myself. Gracias for
guiding me to this house full of fire
alarms that snore through their careers.
I will rescue us from the alphabet of
B films, the lurid paperbacks with
guilty men winking at secret readers,
séances in which we're waiters again.
May I have your address while I'm alive?

Tío, *linda*, queen without expectations
of an empire, you've taught me that
the dead need their sleep too and
that they always dream of humans.

～

Another Ghost

It's years since I have heard
a woman sing for herself,
to herself. This hotel wall
is a porous path to a lady
chapel. I think of Tía Sylvia,
she who sleeps in a forest of
stone forever. How she'd sing
to the few records that she could
afford. Her mouth loved to rule
the musical scale, a kingdom
small enough to sometimes float.
The singer stops and my dead sink.

～

After Sandburg

Construction everywhere: holes full of men
defined by their tools. If only they were
archeologists returning old worlds to us.
But it's Profit that is king here in this
democracy. Lofts after lofts after lofts
perch in the sky, settling into pockets
of blue air. Where will all these tenants
come from? Which towns are being emptied
out? Behind walls of glass are more walls
of glass, glittering fences to keep angels out.
At noon, workers face the lake, that nearby
vastness, that void beyond our machinery.

THE BURRITO KING OF TOLEDO, OHIO

for Maggie Anderson

My father worked in a factory
that had no windows. For years,
he sweated in the bottom of this
abstract ship, never seeing ports,

but always returning to our bills.
He hasn't worked at summing his
life, hasn't worked at titling
his imaginary Selected Poems

as I have: *Midwest Matador,*
or perhaps, *This Country of
Scarecrows.* I'm addicted to dawn,
to light, to vision. I always carry

a notebook with me should anyone
say, this isn't work, this isn't work.
Look, I'll say, I've pages of notes,
most of which will become nothing,

won't become money in the bank.
Perhaps in years, when my poems,
The Burrito King of Toledo, Ohio, is
published, labor will be honored:

mine, my father's. Many days I've
walked into a sea of grass, just
outside of a factory, and have watched
men vanish during shift changes.

It's Dante, imported, more efficient
(no morally exact rhymes to "I'm
fucking tired.") I get to go home with
clean hands, but this worker's shadows

dirty many pages. I've arrived here,
Papi, to this inland embassy, for us,
for when there was an us. Now,
you and your eye-seeing dog try not

to get lost in your Puerto Rico, while
I select new short cuts to get home fast.
The tombstone only offers us breathing
space on its permanent hyphen, island

floating between heaven and hell. It's time
to go through the Taco Bell drive-through,
car blasting Jennifer Lopez's *The Reel Me*.
I give my notebook, and myself, a day off.

LETTER DELIVERED BY THE MOON

Alonso writes on expensive paper he has
saved for years without a reason.

Querido, questioner of questioners,
when did our bed stop being the answers
needed? In lotería dreams, numbers float
like driftwood, innuendos, the black coat that

the moon gives its shadow. But we fell off
the continental drift, salty sailors in love with
themselves more than the sea, the sex, storms.
You're inland now, far from this lighthouse's

winks. You—ringed by cornfields? Farmer's sons?
I still have drafts of your comedy on free will,
Casting Couch Etiquette. Being naked with you
was one way to drown without drowning.

He has no address to put on the envelope.

RUDY

Let's make you a prince fleeing with one carry-on
                    and chipped skis, sconces, scars.
You are given refuge in Utah where everyone is
                    blonde by law and interbreeding.
Hmmn, this poem needs a giant, some Cyclops, a Republican
                    (easy to cast), a wolf, or a lover—yes!
Your lover knows nothing of your birthplace and
                    doesn't believe your stories of the compass
for go-go boys like you are a dime-a-dozen in a mindset
                    that gives billions to charities if they
have the proper breeding. Staying out of sight works
                    for Christmas gifts but not for lovers
seeking swagger and sighting. You, the almost prince,
                    wash dishes, process words, drink.
You work out for that day you'll lead the revolution
                    and for tips that'll cover taking taxis.
You keep waiting for your epic to start a first draft
                    or for angels to maintain your accent.
Waiting is painful because it is the optimist that
                    never goes to a doctor or a priest when ill.
You, the prince, shake your ass to incomplete strangers
                    who think your country exists for vacationers.
In the bedroom closet hangs a raincoat with bullet holes.

IMITATIONS OF BRUCE SPRINGSTEEN

for my lost compañeros

I drove like Magellan
on reds in a maze of ripe
curves, my darkness
more constant than sunrise
and less of an expensive
date. Driving nowhere and
praying to God we'd never
arrive there, Jorge often
rolled down his window
to scream: *There is no Utah.*
Springsteen's "Badlands"
spurred us to own *something*.
We sang along off-key while
throwing our clothes out of
the fast car as if corn silk.

Back to lost Provo, I marvel that
the Saints sleep with their doors
unlocked. The stoned and stunned
still cruise Main Street, just chasing
their own tales. This is my America,
at last, the Mother Lode (*con su
permiso, Señora*), the Big Enchilada.
We race in the street while blasting
"Racing in the Streets." Postmodern
car locos. At secret parties, we are
truths: cowboys seeking straw beds
in which to yield to invisible forces.

The newness of my body over yours
isn't yet a spiritual crisis. As Deidre
points out, drama is dangerous. Ask
the angel Moroni: "Nothing sadder than
empires without forwarding addresses."
What's left of the Spanish conquest of
the Rockies is True Taco, where the illegal
and the immoral sit next to each other
after the Utah bars have squeezed sweat
from us, we who may never know mermen.
Back into the temple of the truck, we drive
without fear on confluent canyon roads.
We loop "Darkness on the Edge of Town"
while burning for the miracle of a city,
ending up far from God and nearer
to motels with morticians on call. Sí,
pull me to you, but understand: to be
stoned alive just takes found stones.

ALWAYS

for Buzz, call me collect

We met in proud Utah and wore opaque
vodka on those vague Sundays for the
unfaithful on your dangling back porch
while dreaming of the very New York

where we entangled for the last time.
Te quiero, you said there, my ears as
paths. You then vanished with a macho
because I had a lover, because we'd

never ride across Russia together in
that frozen train, because listening
to *A Chorus Line* all those weekends
didn't teach us the foreign language

of our bodies, because of your career
as a model after years as a military
mannequin, because we never expected
adios to be our actual parting last word.

Because, because, and because. You
turned around to stare at me and I waved
back: *I love you too.* What an education:
poetry always demands all my ghosts.

WAR CRIMES IN
SODOM & GOMORRAH

Darling, none of these cards are
right: not even the naked carpenter

saying: "your hammer or mine?"
There are few cards for two men sharing

dulling razors. I feel lost in a world so
heterosexual that even mannequins

have the power to judge us, their
private parts neither parts nor private.

WATER FINDS ITS OWN LEVEL
EVEN IN A DESERT:
PALM SPRINGS POEMS

Years after leaving Utah, I'm still
leaving it. This private playground
offers proof to me that I'm no longer that
Mormon elder too young for himself.
Clothing optional doesn't mean soullessness.
It's an adolescent version of owed
adulthood: palm trees with nude tourists
not thinking about God, a guest book
for comments ("my first kiss was
in Room 14"— my room for the week!).
St. Reinaldo Arenas, pleasure isn't
a good widower. More comments: "rain is
coming. Hopefully I well [sic] be soon."
I'm explicit, and like the stewardess
said earlier, easily: "shift happens."
It's amazing that humans love
other human love. On my bed is
a safe-sex kit, bar guides, sun block.
But I came to be seen in this obscene
California light. I sit by the pool, unfazed
by the fact that I'll never be a martyr.

Reading my beloved Shelley, I
envy Lord Byron. Others around
the unblinking pool read of
murder and sex in throwaway
editions of the libido. To be of
this Earth. I'm being stared at:
are secrets showing? showing off?
Naked men are rarely manifestos.
Earlier, I saw a wild rooster in

44

an empty lot. Its plain colors
were mistranslations of Psalms.
My shadow is unshod, unsure.
The erotic publishes books that
use vanishing ink, books of breaths.
Let's go inside, neglect noon, for
we are right: everyone is mysterious.
Without pretense, this hotel room's
painting insists the naked laborer
is more important than St. Mark.
Our own nakedness is one way to talk.
It's true that we gloat about what we
can steal from God. I'm in unholy
Palm Springs where my body has yet
to embrace a man without a gold cross.

Adam's free-range crotch
survives only as a dense book
of dream interpretations:
palm trees in snow means tragic love;
a magic wand means a dark forest:
a city of aching bridges means
some myth is starving to death.
But what of these magnets in skin
lent by sunlight? They—we—
wear warmth in the moonlight,
our solar plexuses as secret suns.
A pool waits to borrow form.
Immanence is always seductive,
the Now as an explicitness. The desert
knows how to flower. Strangers
kiss us back, men freed of contexts.
We're not just ideas—not when we're
clumsy, when offerings are deliberate.

THE DANGERS OF TEQUILA

Enough of it and you are sure
Tijuana is all of Mexico,
that the vertical sailors in

Iguanagila seek your prone
harbor, that your burnished
souvenirs may be antiques soon.

You explain to an egghead fled
from a conference on borders
(whose hotel maid is an illegal)

the significance of Pee Wee Herman
screaming *Tequila!* to bikers.
But how have Sam Shepard's

plays the architecture of true
hangovers? Who isn't a prophet?
You grow too tired for the trolley

back to toothy San Diego. Homeless,
at least intellectually, you seek
tequila underworlds to see if God

sends you a Virgil. Or you may be
someone else's Virgil. Soon, you're
not in Mexico or inside your body.

NORTH, AGAIN

Two Jamaican maids return me North, again,
ask to turn down my bed. No, I'll do it
myself, hermanas. One says, "Your accent?
It's not Spanish, States, or too colonial.

You must move often, son of a sailor?"
How did she know all this from a talk
in my rented doorway? I'm drunk with
the good news, again: I'm negative.

Hola, cruel world! I dress in a black halo
to buy books, to take Keats on a shopping
spree. See all this positive capability?
Streets are full of long angels in leather.

Just last week, I wrote my last will and
testament: I leave the sun, oh, to everyone.
Again, location has little to do with the mind.
The Midwest waits to welcome me back as

a poet wearing a rust belt and not a g-string.
Let it wait as I wear northern sunlight even
if not a spectacle. Being seen is what most
of us comprehend as history. My disposable

camera will dispense flattened shine, later on.
Codicil to my will: I give God my worn shoes.
Horses for tourists on Vieux-Montreal wear
blinders so that forward seems inevitable.

NIGHTS WITHOUT DAWNS

for James Baldwin

A jazz eclipse: we're noisy bar-closers
still unsure that Europe can exist

without our misfortunes of muscles
and mindsets. Music spills like gin.

Echoes scare us, air's cooling cathedrals.
The near gypsies are absent, including

ourselves. The secret saxophones still
feed off generations after generations'

breaths. It's how culture shows up with
cheap luggage, moves in, moves up, is

moved by the idea of youth and youths as
entrees, entries. Better to stumble through

entitled streets as crooked as the teeth of
unowned musicians on stage. The inevitable

flows towards undressings that might or
might not be the nakedness that leads to

kissing a foreigner back who doesn't speak
my earned language, nor I his. The two of

us stare; it's why he religiously pulls down
the shades. We define nations tonight.

FEVER NEAR THE ARCTIC

So I like reckless Reykjavík.
My impression: I'm in
a 501 Jeans wet dream.

Glenn insists that no one can stand
on his head in Iceland—he's right!
My judgment: I'm older. And angry

at Wallace Stevens for having to
invent Europe when it was
waiting for him inside any

footloose camera. This unblinking
hotel is on top of the world;
so there must be a world!

I loudly dreamt last night that
Reinaldo Arenas asked me
to script a dream: *Postcards*

from Sodom and Gomorrah. Today,
Helgi listens to James Brown
before we meet poets and painters

cradling rages inside red beers.
He tells Odin to "make it funky."
The compass will not encompass us.

TINY ITALY

The tenor crowds the room
with his voice, so tiny this Italy.
I see my father's ghost
waiting for me in the garden.

Let him wait. White vases,
white flowers: delicate flames
in a concert hall for a small crowd
in the country. Wine is being

pressed into service, but it's
just stage blood. Father is gone.
I stroll among shy statues.
It can be good to be a stranger.

GREECE, 1910

He seeks British tourists, settles
for French painters who love
order. Later, after the sun
combs its corona, time for

wine offered by the locals.
A mapmaker born centuries
late, he cannot understand
why poets haven't found him.

He is not the one who is lost.
Later, he swims, but drowning
will never be his style: "let
Poseidon crawl for me on shore!"

Somewhere on this island must
be a writer. He waits in darker
bars lit by cigarettes, offering
his specifics and false zodiacs.

FLOWERS IN FLORENCE

Two of the daffodils are dressed
in glowing faces; three of them

grimace in gold masks: resurrection
poses. What's not to love, this

half-spent day? These blossoms are
alternative suns on a cloudy

noon: five sisters gossiping with
spring's army of gray. The astral

plane must be beautiful in order
to tempt some of us from this ache

we call *yellow* that is in and of this
world. These flowers possess the plain

grace of specificity: five
gold coins not long for my cold hands.

MORTALS: LONDON POEMS

How dirty London is this grainy
Ash Wednesday. Papers and
flyers twist and crash while we
with ripping maps seek roads toward
house-broken and poker-faced
palaces. Facets of colonialism
have been turned respectable as
fat museums, harmless graves.
Romanian beggars show undraped
photos of their saintless babies.
Locals clad in black walk with
cell phones, soloists stuck in choirs.
I must choose now: a near pub or
the artistic Apocalypse exhibit?
Cold ale is for us joyful mortals.
In the camaraderie of the dark bar,
I'm losing London while being foolish:
Angel Clare isn't waiting for me still.

What a cliché—a prostitute
in Soho. I ask, "haven't you
ever read Marx?" Shops offer
sex toys without leashes, leather
loincloths, and winks. Back to
my tiny hotel room, I read
frank Frank O'Hara's *Lunch
Poems* (it's where I hide my
Traveler's Checks). He sings
in "Memoir of Sergei O…":
*You are ruining your awful
country and me / it's not new.*
Reading is labor not about pay.

Earlier a stranger sized me up
and handed a card: "you look
like trouble, a dash of *something*."
Invited to a Spice Girl bash,
3 A.M. seems an impossible
starting line. Heaven, the club,
will thrive without my freed
verse. My restlessness isn't
about events or the eventual.
The shower stall is a coffin,
a space shuttle, a fake bullet,
a generic forgiveness of dirt.
I put on my public uniform
of cologne and ignorant jeans.
I'm Pip of *Great Expectations*
pub crawling. My body wants
to be someone else's history.
I'm a new world with condoms,
sideburns and prayers to waste.
This dark city loves its broken heart.

William Blake, the gods punished you
with talent. Poet and painter,
your words hide words in which
a snake coils about a naked
prophet; Abel's body is found;
Christ is a swordsman without
a funny bone. Alpha and Omega
want to own everything, again.
Your "The Ghost of a Flea" predicts
the modern human, Prometheus
forced to go Vegas. A crowd
gathers to see if you'll blink.
You don't. A man with cropped
hair cruises me, but I'm here for

the dark art on the white walls.
Who will box our ears these days?
The meek are incorporated and
the Tiger won't be our messiah
without a golden parachute.
Blake, I say later at The Goose
and Granite, poet, Earth is still
plagued with ghosts and fleas.
I buy rounds but fail to turn us
into illuminated manuscripts.

I'm a tourist without a camera.
Forget St. Paul's and its tired frown,
better this handsome tourist —I must
interrupt this poem but a dwarf just
collapsed! Strangers laugh!—this
handsome tourist who rivals stern
revelations. Let the vague ghosts in
the cathedral pose for 3rd world cameras.
Architecture attempts to own Truth,
get fat on its franchises, prey on the praying.
I've a much closer prophecy. He sees me
seeing him and winks. T.S. Eliot, we
like being human. I ask the stranger his
gray Tuesday's Christian name: *Adam*.
Of course, perfect. An act of God.

Strolling through genteel
gardens contested by dogs,
abandoned suffragettes and
activists with one-cell cell phones.
It's not America I miss, but
Puerto Rico. A passing truck

still blasts Ricky Martin's "Livin'
La Vida Loca." I'm returned to
Bloomsbury where they sell
Virginia Woolf burgers.
I'm dizzy (do men faint?) but change
clothes to meet midnight halfway.
Ricky Martin's crotch is a puzzle
to the purists. Let him enjoy
youth, peddle his aspirations.
It's an age in which brown might not
be a bastard on the color wheel.
Ricky is a bottom on top, trickster
with copyrighted codpiece. Sure, I
wouldn't kick him out of my hammock.
(Empires are ideas first.) Drunk in
Soho, I buy leather pants that cut
my visit down by a week. Still, it's
good to act like my old shoes' I.Q.
and to be younger than my wisdom.
Dawn: a faceless stone mummy blocks
my path. Superstitions trump
my advanced degrees. I retreat,
stumble into the bored Virgin Records'
Superstore and here is Ricky
singing again! Amigo, we're sad
ambassadors from a country
that doesn't exist. Will it ever?

THE MELTING POT BOILS OVER

Certain eccentricities will fade soon enough:
boys named Jesus; Indian cheekbones;
Spanglish as the official language of

any imaginary nation. News this morning:
Jesus is dead in the ancient city of Ur;
his fellow soldiers wear their youth as

rebukes to their elders in secret bunkers.
Dead in the land of the Bible, hermano, ese?
Jesus' Aztec face is returned to us as a ghost

that's American at last, a generic martyr,
a jarhead for all seasons. His familia puts
his photo next to JFK's and the latest popes

who do not speak from the grave about peace.
There are yellow ribbons in trees for the youth,
trees that were once ideal for lyrical lynchings.

THE FLUTE

I follow the sound of a flute to
to a tiny garden wedged between

skyscrapers, an afterthought for
the imaginary public: but we're here.

The flautist offers calm. We don't look
at each other. For a brief time, the eye

is not the guest of honor. Music
hangs between the heavens and Earth.

I bow to the slow moments and then
return to streets hawking headlines

of NASA's budget cuts and of wars with
the terrible percussion of new boots.

LETTER TO A SOLDIER IN IRAQ

We barbecue in your honor, the marinated
as miracles. Your ex is collecting angels,
one way to crowd the mind. My goatee

is gone, leaving just the ghost of my face
in bar mirrors blackening from smoke
without an exit door. Any visits from

Jesus? Buddha? Route 9 is closed so we'll
have to use Shore Road when we hunt new
naked midnights. Prayers are becoming

censors. Been thinking about Judas, how he
was just a bad poker player. Let's envy
rock singers who party in just underwear.

Scholarships are still birthing Republicans.
In your last letter, Iraq seemed a ruin
built on runes. Who wants to die when

there are sins yet to tame? We are polled
as if we can pollinate policies. Imagine:
you with a gun, abs, absolutes. Do you

miss fortune cookies? our illegal swims?
You might die for all this glitter on TV,
celebrities playing bed tag. Please, come

back. Politics is when adrenalin makes one
grab another man, hold him for his truth.
Write when you can, when you can tell.

FAR

Far from the Caribbean, in the beds
of false Apollos, I write of light
long lost to the eyes. Myths are
beggars determined to become family.

Images have to be test-driven, but this
poem isn't a rain forest, no volcano's
blushing lushness. The exiled must
choose between facts and belief: I'm here

—or not here? It depends on the day.
It depends if any day ever exists.
How sad it would be never to have known
palm trees, the sea, the faithless sun.

BOOK SIGNINGS

A handsome man buys my book, asks me to read
his poetry sequence about Pablo Casals that's in
a suitcase in a bus station nest. It's a time when
anyone can be an enemy combatant because
of bad luck—ah, no. I sign my name over and
over again, as if I'm in a killer bee spelling bee.
Why do these hieroglyphics matter to strangers?
I have yet to heal my mirror, much less theirs.

One reader is a chiseled Christian, a library in
tight jeans. Another is Zoroaster just flirting at
a taco stand; he's a new poem waiting a poet.
My exhaustion feels like jet lag without the journey.
I carry a leather notebook—in case of? A poem or
any motorcycle ride out of the mysteries of my myself.
I'm mistaken for Robert Downey, Jr.—in a mug shot?
I sign my books, stop owning them, and mourn later.

I sign, but think of Sandburg's tall Chicago, Hughes' Harlem
of shiny shoes, Arenas' vanishing Cuba, Ritsos' Greece of
erotic ghosts, Hemingway's pubic Paris, Dos Passos' scared
USA, Amichai's unedited Jerusalem, our O'Hara's NY of
"sun-like" Puertorriqueños, Paz's silent Tijuana, Pasolini's Rome
of stigmata feasts, Auden's horsed Iceland, Isherwood's Berlin
in a bad blonde wig, Heaney's mud-fed paradise, Calvino's
floating Italy and Arroyo's—will any place actually be mine?

LEAVING AGAIN

There is no room in my suitcases
for statues from my parents' faith
or a horizon kept from despair
by the movement of seagull mobs.

No, I return home empty-handed,
rehearsal for that slow ride across
the unintelligible River Styx
where even the human body

is left behind to root in the rot.
Sometimes, the sea visits me as if
smuggled, as if an apocryphal
book to memorize to keep it safe

in a library that cannot be torched.
The consuming sea brings no news
of what remains afloat on it.
It has no interest in any kind

of metaphysical drownings and
it withdraws without warning
until I wake up, until I sink in
foreign moonlight even though

logically there is only one moon
that hovers over us like a fate
older than our cosmologies.
Mystery has kingdoms without end.

Most attempts at globality
turn consciousness into commerce.
The regional becomes summary:
the iconic seashell bracelet,

the wayward voodoo lottery god,
the Bacardi rum bottles that
are sold as the sun's alchemists.
My souvenirs? The portable famine,

the dying compass, the absent tide.
After I unpack from my journeys
I get drunk from the weightlessness.
Let fewer commercial maps be drawn

with blank spaces once thought to be lairs
of monsters and non-Christian gods.
Each newer journey dazzles as if a dumb
magnet. I'm often puzzled that what

can be read slowly on a spinning globe
remains abstract, even if visited with
my contemporary flesh and desires.
Writers and readers, why has Sisyphus

stolen the limelight? Again, I unpack
condoms, continents, continuances.
Soon, I repack them. My Caribbean
may never have been mine at all.

I watch strangers changing the time on
watches and I wonder what is unwatched.
Questions have always been feasts.
Leaving again, arrival seems an arrogance.

Rane Arroyo was born in Chicago and began his writing career as a performance artist. He is also a playwright and fiction writer. He received a Ph.D. from the University of Pittsburgh. His awards include the Carl Sandburg Poetry Prize, a Pushcart Prize, the Stonewall Books National Chapbook Prize, The *Sonora Review* Chapbook Award, the George Houston Bass Award for Drama, and the Hart Crane Memorial Award. He is professor of English at the University of Toledo, where he directs the creative writing program.